The Divine Circle

A Poetic Journey of Krishna and His Companions

Ravindra Singh Thakur

Published by
InkQuills Publishing House
www.inkquills.in

First Edition 2024

ISBN: 978-81-967124-9-5

Acknowledgement

Writing "The Divine Circle: A Poetic Journey of Krishna and His Companions" has been a deeply fulfilling and enlightening experience. This book would not have been possible without the guidance, support, and inspiration from many individuals.

First and foremost, I offer my heartfelt gratitude to Lord Krishna, whose divine presence and teachings have been a constant source of inspiration throughout this journey. His stories, miracles, and wisdom have profoundly influenced every poem in this collection.

I extend my sincere thanks to my family and friends, whose unwavering support and encouragement have been invaluable. To my parents, who have always believed in me and my dreams, and to my friends, who have provided constant motivation and feedback – your love and faith have kept me going.

A special thank you to my wife, Kiran, whose love, patience, and understanding have been my anchor throughout this journey. Your unwavering support and belief in me have been the bedrock of this endeavor.

To my little daughter, Vriddhi, whose innocence and joy bring light to my life every day – you are a constant source of inspiration, and this book is dedicated to you with all my love.

I also extend my gratitude to my editor, whose insightful suggestions and meticulous attention to detail have greatly enhanced the quality of this work. Your expertise and dedication have been instrumental in bringing this book to life.

I am deeply grateful to my readers, whose interest and enthusiasm for Krishna's tales have inspired me to delve deeper into these timeless stories. Your support and feedback are greatly appreciated and have driven me to create a work that I hope will resonate with you.

Finally, I would like to acknowledge the countless writers, poets, and scholars whose works on Krishna have enriched my understanding and provided a foundation for this book. Your contributions to the world of literature and spirituality are immensely appreciated.

Thank you all for being a part of this divine journey with me.

With gratitude,
Ravindra Singh Thakur

Dedication

To Lord Krishna, the eternal source of love, wisdom, and inspiration,

And to all those who seek the divine in every moment of life,

This book is dedicated to the timeless stories and teachings that illuminate our paths and to the boundless devotion of Krishna's companions, whose love and faith continue to inspire us.

May the words within these pages bring you closer to the divine circle of Krishna and his beloved friends.

With devotion and gratitude,
Ravindra Singh Thakur

Contents

1. Krishna and Devotees....1

2. Krishna Birth....3

3. Child Krishna....4

4. Krishna and Nand Baba....5

5. Krishna and Yashoda....7

6. Krishna and Vasudev....10

7. Krishna and Devki....12

8. Krishna Flute....14

9. Krishna and Cow....16

10. Krishna and Sandipani Ashram....17

11. Krishna and Sudama....19

12. Krishna and Peacock Feather....21

13. Krishna and Balram....22

14. Krishna and Radha....24

15. Krishna and Barsana....25

16. Krishna and Yamuna....27

17. Krishna Lila....28

18. Krishna and Lalita....29

19. Krishna and Kavita....30

20. Krishna and Subhadra....32

21. Krishna and Gopi....34

22. Krishna and Shreeji....35

23. Krishna and Dwarka....37

24. Krishna and Rukmani......39
25. Krishna and Sudarshan Chakra......41
26. Krishna and Panchjanya Shankh......43
27. Krishna and Mahabharat......45
28. Krishna and Arjun......47
29. Krishna and Draupadi......49
30. Krishna and Yudhisthir......51
31. Krishna and Bhim......53
32. Krishna and Sahdev......55
33. Krishna and Nakul......57
34. Krishna and Kunti......59
35. Krishna and Indraprastha......60
36. Krishna and Duryodhana......62
37.Krishna and Kurukshetra......63
38. Krishna and Karn......65
39. Krishna and Bhishma......66
40. Krishna and Kripacharya......68
41. Krishna and Shishupal......70
42. Krishna and Barbarik......71
43. Krishna and Vidhur......73
44. Krishna Updesh......74
45. Krishna and Drona......76
46. Krishna and Ashwathama......78
47. Krishna and Shikhandi......80
48. Krishna and Sanjay......82

49. Krishna and Abhimanyu 84
50. Krishna and Dhritarashtra..86
51. Krishna and Gandhari..88
52. Krishna is Eternity..90
53. Krishna is Alive Forever..92
54. Krishna's Life After Mahabharat..94
55. Krishna and Hanuman 96
56. Krishna's Wisdom: A Poetic Reflection..98
57. Krishna and Haridas Ji 100
58. Krishna is Immortal..102
59. Krishna and Kripalu Maharaj Ji..104
60. Krishna and Meera 106
61. Krishna and Radha Ramanji..107
62. Krishna and Radha Vallabhacharya Ji..109
63. Krishna and Narad Ji..111
64. Krishna and Mahanbrata Brahmachari 113
65. Krishna and Chaitanya Mahaprabhu 115
66. Krishna and Hridayan Ji 117
67. Krishna and Surdas Ji 119
68. Krishna and Rasdas Ji..121
69. Ode to Krishna Devotees 123
70. Gopal, Our Hearts Delight..125

1. Krishna and Devotees

In Vrindavan's embrace, devotees sway,
To the melody of Krishna, their hearts convey.
Radha's devotion, an eternal flame,
In the cosmic dance, they find their aim.

Bathed in the hues of devotion's delight,
Krishna's devotees, in the moonlit night.
Gopis' footsteps echo on Yamuna's shore,
Their love for the Lord, an endless lore.

With peacock feathers and a flute's sweet sound,
Krishna's devotees, their joy unbound.
From Gokul's meadows to Mathura's grandeur,
They sing His glory, their devotion pure.

In temples adorned with incense and song,
Krishna's devotees, a jubilant throng.
Chanting mantras, with devotion aflame,
In the sacred name, they find their aim.

Through the pages of Bhagavad Gita's grace,
Devotees seek Krishna, their spiritual base.
Arjuna's dilemma, a universal plight,
Krishna's teachings, a beacon of light.

In the tapestry of devotion, colors blend,
Krishna's devotees, with love extend.
From the banks of Yamuna to Dwarka's gate,
They surrender to Krishna, their eternal fate.

In the dance of devotion, a cosmic ballet,
Krishna's devotees, in reverence, sway.
With each prayer, a sacred thread they weave,
In the love of the Lord, their souls believe.

So, let the verses of devotion rise,
Krishna's devotees, with joyous cries.
In Radha's love and Krishna's embrace,
They find eternal bliss, a sacred grace.

2. Krishna Birth

On a dark and stormy night
When the world was filled with fright
A divine child was born
To end the evil and the scorn

He was Krishna, the blue-skinned god
The avatar of Vishnu, the lord of all
He came to Earth with a purpose and a plan
To restore dharma and peace in the land

He grew up in a village of cowherds
With his foster parents and friends
He charmed them all with his playful deeds
And his love that never ends

He lifted mountains, killed demons, and danced with gopis
He taught the Gita, fought the Kauravas, and ruled over Dwarka
He was the hero, the lover, the friend, and the king
He was the source of joy, wisdom, devotion, and everything

He was Krishna, the blue-skinned god
The avatar of Vishnu, the lord of all
He came to Earth with a purpose and a plan
To restore dharma and peace in the land.

3. Child Krishna

He was born in a prison cell
To free the world from evil's spell
He was a joy to his mother's eyes
And a delight to the cowherd's tribe

He loved to play his flute so sweet
And charm the gopis with his feet
He stole the butter from the pots
And made the monkeys his friends and plots

He lifted the mountain on his finger
To save his people from the thunder
He danced with Kaliya in the lake
And made him surrender for his sake

He was the hero of the Mahabharata
And the teacher of the Bhagavad Gita
He was the lord of all creation
And the source of love and devotion

4. Krishna and Nand Baba

In the land of Vrindavan, where love's divine,
There dwelled a father, so gentle, so kind.
Nand, the shepherd, with a heart so light,
Guiding his son, Krishna, through day and night.

With laughter in his eyes and a smile so bright,
Nand taught Krishna about love's endless flight.
He sang songs of joy, with a voice so sweet,
Filling their days with melodies complete.

In the fields of green, they would dance and play,
Chasing butterflies, laughter leading the way.
Nand would spin tales of magical allure,
With Krishna listening, his heart was so pure.

Their bond was unbreakable, a love so deep,
As Nand watched his son, his heart would leap.
He taught young Krishna to tend to the cows,
To care for the land, to honor sacred vows.

With each passing day, their love only grew,
As Nand embraced Krishna, his heart was so true.
Their light-hearted banter filled the air,
A father-son duo, with a love so rare.

Through all the mischief and playful jest,
Nand cherished each moment, feeling so blessed.
He knew that Krishna was destined for more,
But in his heart, he'd always be adored.

So, let us celebrate this bond so pure,
Of Nand and Krishna, their love will endure.
With light-hearted joy, their story we sing,
Father and son, forever connected by love's wing.

5. Krishna and Yashoda

In the lush, green fields of Gokul's heart,
Where rivers of love and devotion start,
There lived a mother, pure and kind,
With a bond divine, two souls entwined.

Yashoda was her name, a mother so dear,
To the playful child she held near,
Krishna, her son, with a radiant glow,
A bond of love they'd forever know.

From dawn's first light to the evening's hush,
Yashoda's love was a tender blush,
In every laugh and every tear,
She stood by Krishna, ever so near.

In fields where cowherds' songs were sung,
Where joy and mischief forever sprung,
Krishna's laughter filled the air,
And Yashoda's heart, without comparison.

When storms of fate did darkly loom,
And shadows threatened joy with gloom,
Yashoda's strength would brightly shine,
A beacon in the dark, divine.

The pots of butter, stolen with glee,
From Yashoda's stores, so full and free,
Were just sweet games to her loving eyes,
For Krishna's joy was her prize.

When demons came with ill intent,
To harm her child, on mischief bent,
Yashoda's faith never did wane,
For in her love, Krishna found no pain.

In dreams she'd see his divine form,
With eyes of love, her heart would warm,
Yet in her arms, he was a child,
Pure and innocent, tender and mild.

Through every scrape and every fall,
Through mischief great and troubles small,
Yashoda's hand was always there,
With tender love, beyond compare.

She'd chase him through the courtyard wide,
With laughter bright, there was no chide,
For every moment, joy or strife,
Was precious in her mother's life.

In stories told by fireside light,
Of Krishna's deeds, of wrong and right,
Yashoda's pride would brightly gleam,
For he was her heart, her soul's sweet dream.

When Krishna's lips blew sweet and low,
The flute's soft tunes that made hearts glow,
Yashoda's eyes would softly close,
Lost in the love that only she knows.

Through forest paths and village ways,
In joyous dance and prayerful praise,

Krishna's every step was blessed,
By Yashoda's love, she gave her best.

As years did pass and time moved on,
And Krishna's duties called at dawn,
Yashoda's heart remained his home,
A sanctuary where he'd freely roam.

For in her arms, he was the world,
A universe of love unfurled,
No matter where his path might lead,
Yashoda's love would always feed.

In Gokul's heart, where stories bloom,
Of endless love, beyond the tomb,
Yashoda and Krishna tale is told,
Of love eternal, pure and bold.

So, let us sing of Yashoda's grace,
Of her steadfast heart and loving embrace,
For in her love, Krishna found his way,
A guiding light, night and day.

In every prayer, in every song,
Their bond of love will linger long,
For Yashoda and her darling child,
Are forever cherished, sweet and mild.

6. Krishna and Vasudev

In the land of Mathura, a tale unfolds,
Of a father's love, a story untold.
Vasudev, the man of virtue and grace,
Whose heart was filled with divine embrace.

With a twinkle in his eyes, he'd watch him play,
His son, the mischievous Krishna, each day.
With a mischievous smile and a flute in hand,
He'd charm the world, like no mortal can.

Oh, Vasudev, the father so wise,
Raised his son under starlit skies.
He taught him the ways of honor and truth,
Guiding him from his tender youth.

Together they'd walk in the fields so green,
Sharing laughter, a sight to be seen.
Krishna, the prankster, would play his tricks,
While Vasudev would marvel at his quick wits.

They'd chase the peacocks in the meadows wide,
Dancing together, side by side.
Their bond, unbreakable, like a sacred thread,
As they laughed and frolicked, their worries shed.

Oh, Vasudev, a father so dear,
His love for Krishna, forever sincere.
He'd sing him lullabies under the moonlit sky,
And Krishna would drift off, with a contented sigh.

With Krishna's birth, Vasudev's heart did swell,
Knowing his son was an incarnation, he could tell.
But in his love, he never let it show,
Treating Krishna as any father would, you know.

So light-hearted was their father-son bond,
A connection that no one could abscond.
Vasudev, the pillar of strength and care,
Nurturing Krishna, beyond compare.

In the annals of time, their story remains,
A father's love, devoid of any chains.
Oh, Vasudev, a light-hearted soul,
Whose love for Krishna will forever console.

7. Krishna and Devki

In the land of Mathura, a mother's love did grow,
Devki, fair and gentle, with a heart all aglow.
Her son, the little Krishna, a mischievous sight,
With a twinkle in his eyes, he filled her days with delight.

Oh, Devki, dear Devki, a mother so divine,
With Krishna by your side, your love would always shine.
From his playful pranks to his charming smile,
You embraced every moment, making life worthwhile.

In the early hours of dawn, as the sun rose high,
Devki would sing her son a lullaby.
With Krishna in her arms, she'd sway to the beat,
A tender serenade, so soothing and sweet.

Oh, Devki, dear Devki, your love knew no bounds,
In Krishna's laughter, pure joy could be found.
From stealing butter to teasing the gopis,
Together, you created cherished memories.

Through the trials and tribulations that life would bring,
Devki stood strong, like a protective wing.
Her light-hearted spirit, a guiding force,
Guiding Krishna's path with love and remorse.

Oh, Devki, dear Devki, a mother so wise,
You nurtured Krishna with love in your eyes.
With every lesson taught and every story told,
You shaped his character, more precious than gold.

In the land of Vrindavan, their bond would bloom,
A mother and son, a love that would consume.
Devki, the light-hearted soul, always there to guide,
As Krishna, the mischievous one, played by her side.

Oh, Devki, dear Devki, a mother so dear,
Your love for Krishna, forever sincere.
In your embrace, he found solace and glee,
A bond that would transcend eternity.

So let us celebrate Devki, the mother so divine,
Whose light-hearted love for Krishna will forever shine.
In their playful moments and tender embrace,
We find the essence of a mother's grace.

8. Krishna Flute

In Vrindavan's groves, where lotuses bloom,
Krishna's flute, a melody to consume.
Carved by celestial hands, with art divine,
A magic wand of music, in Krishna's line.

Held by the lord, with fingers so fair,
The flute's sweet notes, a celestial air.
A symphony that echoed through the night,
In Krishna's lips, a source of delight.

Its dulcet tones, a lullaby to the soul,
Through cosmic dances, its melodies roll.
In Radha's heart, it sparked a flame,
The flute's enchantment, in love's name.

Bansuri, they called it, a celestial reed,
Its resonance, the soul's deepest need.
Played by Krishna, the eternal bard,
In its music, love's journey marred.

Through Vrindavan's fields and Yamuna's shore,
The flute's echo, a tale of yore.
With Gopis dancing, in love's embrace,
Krishna's flute, a divine grace.

In Govardhan's shadow and Nandgaon's hills,
The flute's echo, the heart fulfills.
A call to the cows, a pastoral song,
In Krishna's flute, all hearts belong.

With each breath of life, its notes did weave,
In Krishna's hands, a magic sleeve.
From Raas Leela to the battlefield's hum,
The flute's melody, in every sum.

A symbol of Krishna's divine allure,
The flute's magic, forever pure.
In its music, stories untold,
A tapestry of love, in Krishna's hold.

So in the lore of the divine's pursuit,
Krishna's flute, a celestial loot.
A song of love, in the cosmic spree,
The enchanting saga of bansuri.

9. Krishna and Cow

In the meadows of Vrindavan, Krishna roams,
His laughter echoes, a melody that combs.

With cows by his side, a pastoral delight,
Under the azure sky, a divine daylight.

Krishna, the cowherd, in rapture so deep,
Guiding gentle souls, through pastures they sweep.

Their hooves in rhythm, a dance on the green,
A bond with Krishna, pure and serene.

He tends to their needs with a loving caress,
A shepherd divine, in joyous finesse.

The cows, his companions, in pasture and by stream,
In Krishna's presence, a tranquil dream.

Their eyes mirror devotion, a love untold,
In Krishna's heart, their stories unfold.

Amidst the meadows, a divine connection,
A communion of souls, a divine reflection.

Krishna and cows, a timeless affair,
A pastoral poetry, beyond compare.

10. Krishna and Sandipani Ashram

In the sacred halls of Sandipani's embrace,
Krishna's wisdom blossoms, a celestial grace.

Under the ancient banyan's sheltering arms,
Learning life's lessons, with spiritual charms.

Sandipani Ashram, a haven of ancient lore,
Echoes of Vedic chants, forevermore.

Krishna, the seeker, in quest of profound,
With Sandipani's guidance, wisdom unbound.

In the hallowed corridors, knowledge flows,
As the Ganges of wisdom through time it goes.

Lessons of virtue, in the guru's profound gaze,
Krishna's heart, a sacred flame ablaze.

Friendship and learning intertwine,
In the sanctum of Sandipani's design.

A teacher, a guide, with compassion's hand,
Molding the destiny of the Lord of the land.

With sacred scriptures, the classroom hums,
A symphony of knowledge, where divinity comes.

Sandipani Ashram, a crucible divine,
Where Krishna's brilliance continues to shine.

In the sacred soil, their footsteps entwine,
A legacy of learning, forever in time.

11. Krishna and Sudama

In a village far away, a tale we sing,
Of a friendship that made hearts dance and spring,
Sudama, a humble soul, with dreams so pure,
Embarked on a journey, his heart filled with allure.

With naught but a handful of beaten rice,
He sought his childhood friend, without any vice,
Krishna, the divine, with a heart so kind,
Whose love for Sudama, no distance could bind.

Through fields and forests, Sudama did roam,
With laughter and joy, he felt he was home,
His steps light and airy, like a playful breeze,
His heart filled with hope, as his worries did cease.

In the land of Dwarka, he finally arrived,
To meet his dear Krishna, his soul revived,
But with nothing to offer, he felt quite small,
Would his old friend even recognize him at all?

With a heart full of love, Sudama stood at the gate,
Hesitant and nervous, he prayed for his fate,
But Krishna, the mighty, with eyes so bright,
Embraced Sudama warmly, his friend's pure light.

No treasures or riches, Sudama did possess,
Yet Krishna's love, it knew no bounds, no less,
With laughter and banter, they reminisced,
Of childhood days, filled with mischief and bliss.

The palace walls echoed with their joyous laughter,
As they shared tales of love, both now and thereafter,
Sudama's worries and troubles, they melted away,
In Krishna's friendship, forever they'd stay.

For it's not wealth or status that truly defines,
But the love and laughter, that friendship entwines,
In Sudama's heart, a lesson was learned,
That true friendship is the treasure we yearn.

So let us remember, with hearts light and gay,
The tale of Sudama on that glorious day,
A light-hearted bond, that forever will glow,
Through the sands of time, like a river's flow.

12. Krishna and Peacock Feather

In the realm of tales and vibrant hues,
A peacock feather, Krishna's muse.
Its iridescence, a celestial dance,
Woven in the lore of divine romance.

On Vrindavan's soil, where echoes play,
Krishna, the shepherd, in dharma's array.
A peacock feather adorns his crown,
Symbolizing grace that's widely known.

Feathers shimmer in hues profound,
Each shade is a story, a celestial sound.
Azure whispers of a sacred bond,
Between Krishna and the peacock beyond.

In Yamuna's ripples and Gopis' eyes,
The feather's magic never denies.
A symbol of love, in gardens serene,
Krishna's presence, ethereal and keen.

Dancing through tales, the peacock's grace,
Reflects Krishna's charm, an eternal embrace.
As Radha's devotion, a love divine,
In every plume, their spirits entwine.

So let the poetry unfold, like Krishna's flute,
Notes of peacock feather, resolute.
In Vrindavan's verses, an endless spree,
A dance of love, for eternity.

13. Krishna and Balram

In the realm of tales divine, a bond so true,
Balram and Krishna, brothers through and through.
With hearts so light, they traversed the land,
Hand in hand, a duo so grand.

Balram, the elder, strong and bold,
With muscles of steel, his stories are told.
A farmer, a wrestler, a true blue friend,
His laughter echoes, a joy without end.

With a plough in hand, he tilled the soil,
Sweat on his brow, a hardworking toil.
But amidst the fields, he found delight,
In the simple pleasures, day and night.

His laughter echoed through the fields,
As he wrestled with Krishna, his joy revealed.
Their playful fights, like a dance in the breeze,
Light-hearted banter, putting hearts at ease.

Balram, the protector, a guiding light,
With Krishna by his side, everything felt right.
In their mischievous pranks, they brought laughter,
A bond so strong, it could never shatter.

With a smile on his face, and mischief in his eyes,
Balram charmed all with his clever guise.
He loved his brother, with all his might,
Together they conquered each day and night.

So, let's raise a toast, to Balram so dear,
With his light-hearted spirit, there's nothing to fear.
In tales of love and laughter, he'll forever reside,
A brother to Krishna, a bond that won't subside.

14. Krishna and Radha

In the depths of devotion, there she stands,
Radha, the epitome of love in lands.
Her beauty, pure and divine,
Radiates like a sacred shrine.
With eyes that sparkle like stars at night,
She dances with grace, her movements light.
Her smile, like a blooming flower,
Effortlessly captivates every hour.
In Krishna's embrace, she finds solace,
Their love, a celestial dance, without a trace.
Their hearts entwined, forever entangled,
A love story that will never be unraveled.
Radha, the embodiment of devotion,
Her love for Krishna, an eternal ocean.
She teaches us to love without condition,
To surrender to love's divine mission.
Oh Radha, your love is an inspiration,
A reminder of love's true elevation.
May we all find love, like yours so pure,
And let it guide us, forever secure.

15. Krishna and Barsana

In Barsana's embrace, where love takes flight,
Krishna dances, a divine delight.
Amidst rolling hills and meadows fair,
The playful god, with mischief in the air.

Gopis in colorful garments, hearts aflutter,
Krishna's flute, a soulful, sweet mutter.
Through the streets of Barsana, a joyous parade,
Where love and devotion never fade.

Radha, the queen, with eyes that gleam,
In Barsana's landscapes, a dreamy theme.
Krishna's presence, a celestial rhyme,
Echoes through time, an eternal chime.

In the groves of Vrindavan, where peacocks call,
Krishna and Gopis, a dance enthralls.
Barsana's essence, in every sway,
A tapestry of love, woven each day.

On Yamuna's banks, their stories unfold,
A saga of passion, more precious than gold.
Krishna, the shepherd, in Barsana's lore,
A love so profound, forevermore.

Through the colors of Holi, they unite,
A kaleidoscope of love, pure and bright.
In Barsana's streets, where laughter rings,
Krishna's melody, eternal springs.

So let the poetry of Barsana unfold,
A love story of legends, forever told.
In Krishna's realm, where devotion gleams,
Barsana remains in eternal dreams.

16. Krishna and Yamuna

In Vrindavan's embrace, Krishna danced with delight,
Yamuna's waters shimmered, reflecting moonlight.
Whispers of love echoed along the river's flow,
A divine connection, a mystical, eternal show.

Krishna's laughter, a melody in the night,
Yamuna, a companion, sparkling with pure light.
Lotus blooms adorned the sacred stream,
As love between Krishna and Yamuna did gleam.

Oh, Yamuna, a witness to their celestial affair,
Carrying tales of devotion, beyond compare.
Krishna's playful pranks by the river's side,
Yamuna's waves, like a lover's gentle tide.

Through the verses of time, their tale is spun,
Krishna and Yamuna, forever as one.
In the heart of Vrindavan, where love did deliver,
A timeless saga, Krishna and Yamuna, the eternal river.

17. Krishna Lila

Krishna lila, the divine play
Of the Lord who came to earth one day
To charm the hearts of all who saw
His beauty, grace and love so raw

Krishna lila, the cosmic dance
Of the Lord who showed his transcendence
By lifting mountains, slaying demons
And playing flute with sweetest tunes

Krishna lila, the eternal bliss
Of the Lord who gave his devotees a kiss
By stealing butter, breaking pots
And flirting with the gopis a lot

Krishna lila, the supreme joy
Of the Lord who came as a boy
To reveal the path of bhakti
And fill the world with his glory

18. Krishna and Lalita

Lalita, a companion to Krishna so dear,
In Vrindavan's haven, where love is clear.
Graceful as a peacock in the morning light,
Dancing with Krishna, pure joy taking flight.

Her eyes, like stars, twinkle with devotion,
A friend to Krishna, a soul's sweet potion.
In the Rasa dance, their steps entwine,
Lalita and Krishna, a union divine.

Through the groves of Vrindavan, they roam,
Lalita's laughter, a melody, a celestial poem.
In her presence, Krishna's heart does sway,
A bond eternal, where love holds its sway.

Oh, Lalita, a confidante, a friend so true,
In Krishna's tales, forever woven through.
Together they paint a canvas so bright,
A timeless dance of love, in eternal light.

19. Krishna and Kavita

In the realm of Braj, where devotion blooms,
Radha and Kavita, their love resumes.
A tale untold, in the cosmic spree,
A poetic saga, in eternity.

Radha, the embodiment of love so pure,
In Vrindavan's groves, her love does endure.
With eyes like lotus, and a heart aglow,
In Krishna's presence, her emotions flow.

Kavita, a poetess with verses divine,
Her words like music, in Krishna's design.
Through the art of expression, a love untold,
In the verses of Kavita, emotions unfold.

Radha's love, a celestial flame,
In the cosmic dance, where emotions claim.
With the fragrance of jasmine and the peacock's plume,
Radha and Kavita, in love's sweet bloom.

Through the meadows of Braj, where Krishna treads,
Radha's heart in Kavita's verses spreads.
A poetic canvas, where emotions paint,
In the realm of love, no restraint.

Kavita's words, like a gentle breeze,
In Radha's heart, a love that appease.
With ink and quill, emotions entwine,
A poet's devotion, like the divine.

Through moonlit nights and sunlit days,
Radha and Kavita, in love's maze.
A dance of words, a cosmic rhyme,
In the heart of Braj, love does chime.

Radha's love, a spiritual quest,
In Kavita's verses, emotions expressed.
A tale of devotion, in every line,
In the cosmic tapestry, their love does shine.

So in the verses of Braj's lyrical song,
Radha and Kavita, forever strong.
A poetic saga, in eternity,
Their love's resonance, a cosmic symphony.

20. Krishna and Subhadra

In the realm of divine love, Krishna and Subhadra dance,
A celestial romance, a symphony of chance.

Krishna, the enchanting flute player so divine,
Captivating hearts, a melody entwined.

Subhadra, with grace in every step she takes,
Her love for Krishna, an eternal bond that awakes.

Under the moonlit sky, they share a cosmic embrace,
A celestial ballet, transcending time and space.

In Vrindavan's groves, their love blooms like flowers,
An eternal connection, beyond earthly hours.

Subhadra's eyes, pools of love so deep,
In Krishna's heart, her name, a secret he keeps.

Together they sway, in the dance of devotion,
A divine partnership, a timeless ocean.

Krishna's flute echoes through the divine air,
A symphony of love, beyond compare.

Subhadra, the sister of Balarama so dear,
In Krishna's presence, she feels no fear.

In Dwaraka's palaces, their love story unfolds,
A tapestry of emotions, in the fabric of time it molds.

Through trials and triumphs, their bond only grows,
A love that eternity in its essence knows.

So let the verses sing of Krishna and Subhadra,
A celestial saga, a love that transcends para.

21. Krishna and Gopi

In the realm of devotion, the Gopis reside,
With love for Krishna, their hearts are tied.
In Vrindavan's meadows, they dance and play,
Lost in love's ecstasy, throughout the day.
Their souls aflame with devotion's fire,
Their love for Krishna, the ultimate desire.
With every step, they follow his divine flute,
Their hearts intertwined; in love they are mute.
Their love, selfless and pure as can be,
They surrender completely, for all to see.
Through tests and trials, their love remains steadfast,
In Krishna's embrace, their souls find rest.
In their hearts, Krishna forever resides,
Their love for him, no boundaries or divides.
They are the embodiment of devotion's might,
Radiating love, like stars in the night.
Oh, Gopis, your love an eternal flame,
An inspiration to all, in Krishna's name.
May we too, like you, find love's embrace,
And experience divine bliss and grace.
In the realm of devotion, the Gopis show,
That love for the divine, is the way to grow.
With hearts open wide, let us follow their lead,
And dance in love's ecstasy, fulfilling every need

22. Krishna and Shreeji

In Vrindavan's groves, where lotuses bloom,
Krishna Shree Ji, in divine costume.
A lord of love, with a peacock feathered crown,
In every heart, his presence renowned.

A flute in hand, its melodies so sweet,
In Krishna's music, all souls meet.
Through Yamuna's waves and Govardhan's embrace,
Krishna's divinity, a timeless grace.

In Gokul's lanes, where the cows did graze,
Krishna's childhood, in the sunlight's blaze.
A mischievous smile, a twinkle in his eye,
In Krishna's leelas, the cosmic sky.

From the serpent's dance to the butter's heist,
Krishna's childhood, in stories spiced.
Yashoda's love, like an endless stream,
In Krishna's heart, a maternal dream.

As Radha's beloved, in the rasa dance,
Krishna's love, a divine trance.
Through the melodies of Vrindavan's song,
In Krishna's embrace, love's journey long.

To Mathura's city, he rode in might,
With Kansa's defeat, a cosmic sight.
Dwarka's kingdom, where oceans meet,
In Krishna's rule, a love so sweet.

The Bhagavad Gita, his teachings profound,
In Kurukshetra's field, where battles resound.
Arjuna's guide, in wisdom's embrace,
Krishna Shree Ji, a cosmic grace.

Through cosmic dances and tales untold,
Krishna's saga, in scriptures unfold.
A lord of compassion, a friend so dear,
In every devotee's heart, Krishna's cheer.

So in the cosmic tapestry, where stories weave,
Krishna Shree Ji, in hearts does cleave.
A symbol of love, a timeless spree,
In Krishna's grace, eternally.

23. Krishna and Dwarka

In Dwarka's realm, where waves caress the shore,
Krishna, the divine, his presence evermore.
A city of opulence, in ocean's embrace,
Dwarka's splendor, a celestial grace.

Built by Vishwakarma, the celestial art,
Dwarka stood as Krishna's own heart.
Palaces of gold and jewels so bright,
A kingdom resplendent in Krishna's light.

Yadavas thrived in this city grand,
Under Krishna's rule, a blissful land.
Dharma's protector, a compassionate king,
In Dwarka's haven, love took wing.

The conch's melodious call echoed wide,
In Dwarka's streets, where joy did bide.
With Sudarshan chakra, Krishna's might,
A sovereign ruler, in truth and right.

In the heart of Dwarka, a temple divine,
Krishna worshipped, in devotion's shrine.
With Rukmini by his side, love's flame,
In Dwarka's sanctuary, they eternally claim.

Yet shadows loomed, as destiny played its part,
The great war of Kurukshetra, where it did start.
Krishna's wisdom, a guiding light,
In the epic's tapestry, a celestial fight.

Dwarka's demise, in the ocean's swirl,
A cosmic event, where oceans twirl.
Yet Krishna's legacy, beyond the flood,
In devotees' hearts, like a sacred bud.

The city of Dwarka, though lost to the sea,
In Krishna's stories, it forever be.
A kingdom of love, beyond time's sway,
In Dwarka's tales, Krishna holds his sway.

So, in the echoes of Dwarka's lore,
Krishna's presence, we forever adore.
In the cosmic dance, where stories unfurl,
Dwarka remains, in Krishna's eternal.

24. Krishna and Rukmani

In Vrindavan's embrace, where peacocks dance,
The flute's sweet melody, a divine romance.
Krishna, the eternal, with charm untold,
Stories of love and valor, through ages unfold.

In Dwarka's city, where oceans kiss the shore,
Rukmini, a queen, her beauty evermore.
A princess adorned with grace and charm,
In Krishna's heart, she held a sacred balm.

A love story etched in tales of yore,
Krishna and Rukmini, forevermore.
From her palace chamber, a plea took flight,
To Krishna, the beacon of love's pure light.

In a missive sent, with words sincere,
Rukmini poured her heart, devoid of fear.
A plea for rescue from an unwanted fate,
In Krishna's love, she sought her state.

A divine chariot, to the rescue sped,
As vows were taken, and promises led.
Away from the palace, love's daring flight,
Krishna and Rukmini, in the moonlit night.

Through mystical forests and moonlit streams,
In the realm of love, where reality teems.
Rukmini's heart, with devotion ablaze,
In Krishna's arms, a sanctuary she lays.

Together they danced, in love's euphoric trance,
A celestial union, a divine romance.
Krishna, the lord, and Rukmini, his queen,
In love's tapestry, forever seen.

Dwarka's kingdom, where they reigned,
Through joy and sorrow, love remained.
Rukmini, by Krishna's side so true,
In their eternal love, they forever grew.

In tales of devotion, their love persists,
Krishna and Rukmini, where bliss exists.
A saga of love, painted in hues divine,
In the cosmic canvas, their spirits entwine.

25. Krishna and Sudarshan Chakra

In Krishna's hand, a disc of flame,
Sudarshan Chakra, with cosmic aim.
A celestial wheel, in brilliance spun,
In the cosmic tapestry, its battles won.

Forged by divine hands, in sacred fire,
Sudarshan Chakra, a cosmic lyre.
A weapon of time, with edges keen,
In Krishna's grip, its power unseen.

A symbol of dharma, righteous might,
Sudarshan's glow, in the darkest night.
Spinning with speed, a cosmic dance,
In the face of evil, a formidable lance.

In Kurukshetra's field, its blades did gleam,
Sudarshan Chakra, in a righteous scheme.
Defending truth, cutting through the night,
A divine weapon, in Krishna's light.

Through battles fierce, its path was traced,
Sudarshan's justice, in war embraced.
A wheel of time, with destiny entwined,
In Krishna's hands, its purpose defined.

Protected the devotees, the virtuous heart,
Sudarshan Chakra, a work of art.
With a hum of power, like cosmic hymns,
It vanquished foes, in Krishna's whims.

Yet in its might, a message profound,
Sudarshan's mercy, in its whirling sound.
A cosmic cycle, life and death,
In Krishna's love, its eternal breath.

So in the lore of Sudarshan's blaze,
A weapon of righteousness, in time's maze.
A wheel of destiny, in Krishna's care,
Sudarshan Chakra, a cosmic flare.

26. Krishna and Panchjanya Shankh

In the celestial realms, where stories entwine,
Krishna's conch, Panchajanya, divine.
A sacred shankh, with history profound,
Echoes of battles in its resounding sound.

From the ocean's depths, a mystic birth,
Panchajanya emerged, a conch of worth.
In Krishna's grip, a symbol of might,
As he stood, a beacon in Kurukshetra's fight.

With a mighty blow, the shankh did roar,
Its sound resonating, an eternal lore.
Announcing war's onset, a cosmic decree,
Panchajanya heralded destiny.

In Dwaraka's city, by the ocean's swell,
Panchajanya's tales, in Krishna's shell.
A symbol of victory, in every war,
Its echo a hymn, like never before.

When Krishna blew, the Panchajanya shell,
Kauravas trembled, in that war-torn swell.
Guiding Arjuna, with words of might,
Krishna wielded Panchajanya, a celestial light.

A conch that echoed through Dvapara's air,
Panchajanya's sound, a signal rare.
From Kurukshetra's plains to Dwarka's shore,
Its resounding call, a lore evermore.

In Krishna's hands, the Panchajanya gleams,
A symbol of conquest, in cosmic dreams.
With its echoes, tales of valor unfold,
In battles fought, and epics told.

So in the saga of Krishna's divine dance,
Panchajanya's resonance, a cosmic trance.
A conch of destiny, in Krishna's sway,
Its hymns in time's echoes, forever stay.

27. Krishna and Mahabharat

In the land where legends unfold,
A tapestry of stories, timeless and bold.

In Hastinapura's regal hall,
Mahabharata's epic, a tale enthralled.

Kings and queens, warriors so grand,
A cosmic drama, destiny's hand.

At the heart of it all, Krishna divine,
A charioteer, a friend benign.

Arjuna, with bow and arrow in hand,
Faced dilemmas in a war-torn land.

The Pandavas, bound by kin,
Draupadi's laughter, a joyous din.

Yet, dice rolled fate's cruel game,
A kingdom lost, in fortune's name.

Through the forest of exile they roamed,
In shadows and echoes, destinies combed.

Draupadi's honor, a dice's cruel jest,
A vow sworn in her heart's unrest.

Krishna's counsel, a cosmic guide,
In the river of duty, they did abide.

Bhishma's oath, steadfast and true,
A sacrifice grand, in the morning dew.

Karna, noble yet misunderstood,
Destiny's child, in shadows he stood.

In Kurukshetra, the battle's roar,
Echoed truths and tales galore.

Chariots clashed and arrows flew,
As time itself, the epic grew.

Drona's prowess, a teacher's might,
As warriors fell in the cosmic fight.

Abhimanyu, a youth so brave,
In the chakravyuha, found a hero's grave.

Krishna's discourse, the Bhagavad Gita,
Wisdom profound, a cosmic vista.

Yudhishthira's dilemmas, right and wrong,
In the cosmic dance, a ceaseless song.

At last, the war's tumultuous tide,
On the field of Kurukshetra, heroes bide.

Victory and loss, intertwined fate,
As the epic closes its cosmic gate.

In Mahabharata's echoes, stories untold,
Krishna's flute plays, a tale manifold.

28. Krishna and Arjun

Upon Kurukshetra's vast expanse,
Two souls entwined in fate's own dance.
Krishna and Arjun, a divine pair,
In the epic tale, a bond so rare.

The charioteer of wisdom, Lord so kind,
Krishna guides Arjun, the conflicted mind.
Amidst the battle's clamor and strife,
He imparts the teachings that transcend life.

With a cosmic vision, Krishna reveals,
The truth of existence, the heart heals.
Arjun, torn in doubt and despair,
Finds solace in Krishna's words, a prayer.

In the discourse of Bhagavad Gita's song,
The wisdom flows, profound and strong.
Duty, righteousness, paths to tread,
Krishna's guidance, a light to be led.

On the battlefield, where destinies collide,
Arjun seeks counsel in Krishna's stride.
With chariot wheels and conch shell's call,
They stand united, amidst chaos tall.

The celestial discourse, a cosmic conversation,
Krishna unveils the path of salvation.
Arjun, the seeker, in contemplation deep,
Embraces Krishna's words, his soul to keep.

Through the trials of life, in joy or strife,
Krishna and Arjun, the eternal life.
A bond unbroken, a friendship divine,
In the tapestry of time, their spirits entwine.

So, in the verses of the Mahabharata's art,
Krishna and Arjun, never apart.
In duty, in love, in battles fought,
Their saga echoes, lessons taught.

29. Krishna and Draupadi

In the tapestry of Mahabharata's epic grace,
A tale unfolds, Krishna and Draupadi embrace.

Draupadi, born from the sacred fire's dance,
An embodiment of beauty, destiny's chance.

Krishna, the divine guide in cosmic hues,
With his wisdom profound, life he imbues.

Draupadi's swayamvara, a pivotal scene,
Arjuna's prowess, a warrior's sheen.

Yet, destiny's twist, a polyandrous fate,
Five Pandavas, in love, would participate.

Krishna, the charioteer of Arjuna's plight,
Guiding him through dharma's cosmic light.

Draupadi's laughter, a cascade of grace,
In Hastinapura's corridors, she found her place.

Through the dice's cruel game, a kingdom lost,
Draupadi's honor, at an unfathomable cost.

Krishna, the eternal friend, a solace near,
His presence, a balm, in times of fear.

The vastraharan, a moment intense,
Draupadi's plea, a divine defense.

In exile's shadows and forest's embrace,
Krishna and Draupadi, sharing life's space.

Through trials and tribulations, their bond unwavering,
In Kurukshetra's storm, destiny engraving.

Krishna's divine discourse, Bhagavad Gita's song,
A cosmic revelation, life's path strong.

Draupadi, resilient in adversities' spree,
Her strength and grace, a timeless decree.

In the Mahabharata's pages, their stories entwine,
Krishna and Draupadi, a saga divine.

30. Krishna and Yudhisthir

In the grand halls of Hastinapura's might,
A saga unfolds, in history's light.
Yudhishthir, noble in his reign,
A king with virtue, a sovereign's gain.

Guided by Dharma, his righteous guide,
Yudhishthir treads where destinies bide.
Through trials and tribulations, a royal stride,
Krishna walks with him, by his side.

In the corridors of Kurukshetra's fate,
Krishna and Yudhishthir, a bond innate.
The charioteer divine, the sage profound,
In the battlefield's chaos, their truths resound.

Through the dice's play, a kingdom lost,
Yudhishthir bears the burdens, the ultimate cost.
Yet, Krishna's counsel, a guiding flame,
In the cosmic drama, they play the game.

A tale of righteousness, in Mahabharata's rhyme,
Krishna and Yudhishthir, through space and time.
In the halls of righteousness, where justice rings,
Their alliance echoes, like celestial wings.

Yudhishthir's queries, Krishna does unfold,
In wisdom's embrace, their stories told.
Duty, righteousness, and life's profound quest,
In the verses scripted, their virtues rest.

So, in the annals of epic lore,
Krishna and Yudhishthir, forevermore.
In the cosmic tapestry, their tales align,
A union of virtue, a bond divine.

31. Krishna and Bhim

In the realm of Kurukshetra's vast expanse,
A tale of brothers, a bond to enhance.
Bhim, mighty in strength, a force untamed,
Krishna walks with him, their destinies named.

With muscles like mountains, and heart so bold,
Bhim's saga, in Mahabharata, unfolds.
Krishna, the charioteer, in battles dire,
Guides Bhim's might, with a celestial fire.

In Draupadi's swayamvara, a lion's roar,
Bhim's strength displayed, forevermore.
Krishna, the witness, to vows profound,
In brotherhood's circle, their bonds are bound.

Through forests dense and trials severe,
Bhim and Krishna, a camaraderie dear.
In exile's hardship, through the darkest night,
Bhim's devotion to Krishna burns bright.

On Kurukshetra's field, where armies collide,
Bhim's valor, in Krishna's stride.
A mace's swing, a thunderous sound,
Krishna's guidance, in victory crowned.

Through Kaurava's arrogance and deceit,
Bhim's wrath, in Krishna's heartbeat.
In the dice's play, and the oath they swore,
Krishna and Bhim, their destinies explore.

In tales of might, and brotherhood true,
Krishna and Bhim, an eternal view.
Through the pages of time, where legends spin,
Their saga resonates, like a cosmic hymn.

So, in the tapestry of Mahabharata's art,
Bhim and Krishna, never apart.
In battles waged and victories won,
Their brotherhood echoes, like the morning sun.

32. Krishna and Sahdev

In the lineage of Pandu, a noble son,
Sahdev, his journey, just begun.
A prince of virtue, in Mahabharata's scroll,
His tale unfolds with Krishna's soul.

Amidst the Pandavas, a brother true,
Sahdev's character, like morning dew.
With Krishna's wisdom, in friendship tight,
A bond that echoes in eternal light.

In Khandavaprastha's realm so grand,
Sahdev's skills, like grains of sand.
Krishna, the guide, in wisdom's sway,
Sahdev walks the righteous way.

A master of steeds, a warrior's art,
Sahdev's valor, a beating heart.
In the cosmic play, where destinies dance,
Krishna and Sahdev, in a timeless trance.

In the dice's play, where shadows fall,
Sahdev faces destiny, standing tall.
With Krishna's grace, a steady hand,
In the face of adversity, Sahdev withstand.

Through the vows they swore, in sacred fire,
Sahdev and Krishna, their destinies aspire.
In the tapestry of time, where legends entwine,
Their saga echoes, a celestial sign.

So, in the verses of ancient lore,
Sahdev and Krishna, forevermore.
In battles waged and victories won,
Their tale unfolds, like the morning sun.

33. Krishna and Nakul

In the land of Hastinapura's royal grace,
Nakul, a prince with a noble trace.
A son of Pandu, with lineage divine,
His tale entwined with Krishna's design.

With a radiant charm and skills refined,
Nakul's presence, like the sweetest wind.
Amidst the Pandavas, a brother true,
In Krishna's embrace, his virtues grew.

In Khandavaprastha's kingdom of yore,
Nakul's valor, like a lion's roar.
Krishna, the guide, in wisdom's sway,
Nakul walks the righteous way.

A master in arts, a horseman bold,
Nakul's tales in Mahabharata unfold.
Krishna, the charioteer, in battles grand,
Nakul fights, with a noble stand.

In the dice's play, where shadows loom,
Nakul faces destiny, in the palace's gloom.
Krishna's counsel, a beacon's light,
In the darkest hours, a warrior's fight.

Through the vows they swore, in the sacred fire,
Nakul and Krishna, their destinies aspire.
In the tapestry of time, where legends entwine,
Their saga echoes, a celestial sign.

So, in the verses of the ancient lore,
Nakul and Krishna, forevermore.
In battles waged and victories won,
Their tale unfolds, like the morning sun.

34. Krishna and Kunti

Kunti, a mother with a heart so pure,
In Krishna's love, she found the cure.
A queen by birth, yet fate's design,
In life's tapestry, Krishna's light would shine.

With secret prayers, a boon she gained,
Summoning Krishna when life's trials pained.
In Draupadi's swayamvara, destiny's play,
Krishna stood by her, guiding the way.

Kunti, wise in love, and sorrow's touch,
Krishna's teachings she cherished much.
Through Kurukshetra's fierce battlefield,
Krishna's counsel, her spirit would wield.

A bond beyond kinship, a soulful tie,
Kunti and Krishna, under destiny's sky.
Through joys and sorrows, a journey untold,
In Krishna's love, Kunti's heart did unfold.

In the Mahabharata's pages, their stories entwine,
Kunti, a devotee, in Krishna's light did shine.
A mother's love, a celestial art,
In Krishna's embrace, eternally a part.

35. Krishna and Indraprastha

In the ancient realm of Indraprastha's grace,
A city adorned, a celestial embrace.
Krishna, the divine, in Dvapara's prime,
A tale unfolds, beyond space and time.

Pandavas' capital, with splendor untold,
Indraprastha's glory, a saga bold.
Krishna, the guide, with wisdom profound,
In the city's heart, love's stories resound.

Built by divine architects, a city grand,
In Indraprastha's streets, destiny planned.
Yudhishthira's rule, just and fair,
A kingdom where justice filled the air.

Krishna, the friend, in every trial,
Through joy and sorrow, mile by mile.
In the palace halls, where intrigue did play,
Krishna's counsel, a guiding ray.

The dice's game, a twist of fate,
Draupadi's plight, sealed by hate.
Krishna's intervention, a miracle spun,
In Kunti's sons' hearts, the battles begun.

In the Rajasuya Yajna's grandeur,
Indraprastha shone, a city pure.
Krishna's presence, a divine grace,
In the tapestry of time, a sacred trace.

In the great war of Kurukshetra's land,
Krishna stood by, with a steadfast hand.
The Bhagavad Gita, a celestial song,
In Indraprastha's echoes, its verses throng.

Post-war, in Hastinapura's throne,
Yudhishthira ruled, but not alone.
With Krishna's friendship, a bond so tight,
In Indraprastha's realm, a guiding light.

As the epic tale draws to a close,
In Indraprastha's history, Krishna chose.
A city of virtue, where dharma prevailed,
In Krishna's love, the saga hailed.

So in the annals of Indraprastha's lore,
Krishna's presence, forevermore.
A city of righteousness, where legends play,
In Krishna's embrace, its echoes stay.

36. Krishna and Duryodhana

In the halls of Kurukshetra, a tale of two,
Krishna and Duryodhana, perspectives askew.
One, the embodiment of divine grace,
The other, entangled in power's embrace.

Duryodhana, driven by ambition's fire,
Krishna's warnings, he chose to dire.
Blinded by ego, on a perilous quest,
He sought power, but love he suppressed.

Krishna's counsel, a beacon in the night,
Duryodhana's heart veiled in shadows, not light.
A battlefield's stage, their destinies entwined,
Krishna's compassion against Duryodhana's mind.

Amidst the clash of warriors and war's cruel song,
Duryodhana's choices, a path gone wrong.
Krishna's presence, a cosmic decree,
A lesson in karma, for all to see.

In the Mahabharata's echoes, their stories align,
Krishna's love enduring, Duryodhana's decline.
A saga unfolds, in time's relentless span,
Krishna and Duryodhana, intertwined, yet ran.

37.Krishna and Kurukshetra

Kurukshetra, a land of ancient tales,
Where warriors clashed, and destiny set its sails.
A canvas painted with valor and might,
Where heroes fought under the sun's golden light.

In this realm of battles and strife,
I find a spark of light-hearted life.
Amidst the chaos and the war's cruel play,
There's laughter that dances, chasing worries away.

The air is alive with jovial cheer,
As soldiers gather, their spirits sincere.
They jest and they banter, with a playful grin,
For in Kurukshetra, joy can always begin.

The warriors, with hearts as strong as steel,
Find solace in moments that laughter can heal.
Their camaraderie, a bond unbreakable,
A testament to the spirit unshakeable.

Here, amidst the clatter of swords and spears,
Laughter echoes, soothing battle-worn fears.
For even in the darkest of times, they know,
That light-heartedness can help their spirits grow.

In Kurukshetra's vast and hallowed ground,
Mirth and joy are the treasures found.
For amidst the chaos and the battlefield's strife,
Laughter becomes the elixir of life.

So, let us celebrate this land so grand,
Where light-heartedness takes a noble stand.
In Kurukshetra, where courage and joy reside,
The warriors find solace, side by side.

38. Krishna and Karn

In the sands of destiny, Krishna and Karn,
Two souls entwined; their fates drawn.

Karn, the sunlit warrior with a heart sincere,
His loyalty tested, destiny's frontier.

Krishna, the cosmic guide, with wisdom profound,
Nurturing virtues on life's battleground.

Karn's golden armor, a symbol of might,
Yet within, shadows of an inner fight.

Krishna's words, a celestial light,
Guiding Karn through the darkest night.

Friend and foe, a tale bittersweet,
Karn's noble heart, Krishna's rhythmic beat.

On Kurukshetra's canvas, destiny unfurls,
Krishna and Karn, in life's swirling whirls.

Through the echoes of chariots and the clash of swords,
Their bond endures, in eternal chords.

39. Krishna and Bhishma

In the twilight of Kurukshetra, where destinies entwine,
Krishna, the charioteer, in cosmic design.
Bhishma, the grandsire, with valor untold,
In the epic saga, their stories unfold.

On the battlefield, where conch shells resound,
Krishna guides Arjuna, wisdom profound.
Bhishma, the stalwart, in his solemn vow,
To protect Kuru's throne, no matter how.

With the sun as witness, and war cries loud,
Krishna imparts lessons, a celestial shroud.
In the chariot's embrace, as wheels turn fate,
He steers Arjuna through karma's gate.

Bhishma, the commander, arrows like rain,
A warrior's honor, in every vein.
Yet Krishna's presence, a divine chore,
Navigating the dharma, at Kurukshetra's core.

The sun retreats, shadows lengthen the strife,
Arrows and mantras in the dance of life.
Krishna's discourse, a beacon so bright,
Illuminates the path, in the war's dark night.

Bhishma, on his bed of arrows, serene,
His sacrifice, a testament unseen.
The battlefield weeps, as warriors fall,
Krishna's mercy, encompassing all.

In the cosmic chess game, where pawns move,
Krishna and Bhishma, destiny they prove.
A war of righteousness, a moral quest,
Where hearts are tested, in every chest.

As the curtain descends on Kurukshetra's stage,
Krishna's wisdom echoes through every age.
Bhishma's sacrifice, a lesson profound,
In the annals of time, their stories resound.

40. Krishna and Kripacharya

In the epic of Mahabharata, where destinies entwine,
Two souls emerge, Krishna and Kripacharya, in a cosmic design.

Kripacharya, a noble sage of lineage divine,
With knowledge vast and wisdom's radiant shine.

Guiding the Kuru clan with his virtuous might,
A mentor revered, in the realm of day and night.

Krishna, the enigmatic charioteer of Arjuna's quest,
In the cosmic drama, orchestrating destiny's test.

Kripa, a stalwart in the Kurukshetra war,
A tapestry of honor and duty, deep at its core.

Krishna, with a flute and a mesmerizing smile,
Kripacharya, with dharma's teachings, versatile.

On the battlefield, where righteousness contends,
Krishna's guidance, Kripa's wisdom blends.

In the court of Hastinapura, where shadows loom,
Kripacharya imparts counsel, dispelling the gloom.

As arrows rain down and the war drums beat,
Krishna and Kripa, a saga so complete.

Krishna, the charioteer, steering the cosmic wheel,
Kripacharya, with ethics and valor, a luminous seal.

Their destinies intertwined, in the cosmic array,
Through righteousness and duty, they pave the way.

In the echoes of Kurukshetra, their tales persist,
Krishna and Kripacharya, in the epic's twist.

So let the verses sing of their valor and might,
In the timeless tapestry, where darkness meets light.

41. Krishna and Shishupal

Shishupala, a soul with envy ablaze,
In Krishna's presence, a tumultuous phase.
Jealousy's flames, a consuming fire,
Yet Krishna's grace, a divine lyre.

In the royal court, where disdain took flight,
Shishupala challenged Krishna's might.
Counting offenses, his rage unfurled,
Yet Krishna's patience embraced the world.

Krishna, the beacon of cosmic grace,
Enduring Shishupala's anger's embrace.
The final count reached, a hundred offenses told,
Krishna's Sudarshana, destiny's unfold.

Shishupala's demise, a cosmic decree,
In Krishna's presence, all souls set free.
The wheel of time turned, in justice's spin,
A tale of redemption, where love could begin.

Oh, Shishupala, lost in envy's flame,
Yet Krishna's mercy, a divine aim.
In the cosmic dance, where destinies twirl,
A lesson unfolds, in the grand, eternal swirl.

42. Krishna and Barbarik

In the annals of time, where legends are spun,
Two souls emerge, a tale begun.
Krishna, the lord with a cosmic gaze,
And Barbarik, a warrior in ancient days.

Krishna, the divine, in Vrindavan's land,
A mystic figure, with a flute in hand.
In Mathura's streets and Dwarka's grace,
Krishna's presence, a celestial embrace.

Barbarik, a hero of the Kuru kin,
Endowed with might, a spirit within.
A bowman supreme, in his youth,
His prowess sung, a tale uncouth.

In the Mahabharata's grand design,
Krishna's wisdom, a beacon so fine.
As Arjuna's guide on Kurukshetra's plain,
In the cosmic dance, he did reign.

On the other side, Barbarik stood,
A warrior fierce, in the Kuru brotherhood.
A pledge he made, to witness all,
With three arrows, a vow so tall.

The divine contest, the great debate,
Barbarik's words, sealed his fate.
Krishna, the master, in strategy's lore,
Barbarik's pledge, he could explore.

A single leaf from a tree nearby,
Barbarik aimed, and let it fly.
As Krishna's toe stopped the leaf with ease,
Barbarik saw, his vow to appease.

In awe of Krishna's cosmic might,
Barbarik surrendered, in that divine light.
With devotion pure, to Krishna's charm,
He offered his head, a sacred balm.

Barbarik's sacrifice, a lesson grand,
In Krishna's play, as fate was planned.
A witness silent, in the battle's roar,
His spirit lives on, forevermore.

So in the cosmic tale of Krishna's sway,
And Barbarik's valor, in that array.
Two souls entwined, in the epic's spree,
A timeless saga, in eternity.

43. Krishna and Vidhur

Vidura, a sage in the court's disguise,
In Krishna's presence, wisdom did arise.
A voice of reason in Kaurava's reign,
Krishna and Vidura, a cosmic refrain.

Guided by dharma, Vidura stood strong,
Injustice challenged, with truth as his song.
Krishna's ally, in virtue's embrace,
A steady presence in life's complex maze.

Through Kurukshetra's shadows, Vidura walked,
In Krishna's wisdom, truth and justice talked.
A counsel profound, in the palace's hall,
Vidura echoed the divine call.

Krishna and Vidura, a bond unseen,
In the corridors of power, where plots convene.
Amidst intrigues and Kaurava's strife,
Vidura sought a righteous life.

In the pages of Mahabharata's lore,
Vidura's wisdom, forevermore.
A sage, a friend, in Krishna's grand plan,
Vidura and Krishna, in life's eternal span.

44. Krishna Updesh

In the realm of Kurukshetra, where destiny unfolds,
Krishna speaks, His wisdom, a tale retold.
The charioteer divine, with Arjun at his side,
Bhagavad Gita's verses, a spiritual guide.

"Arise, O Arjun," in battle's fierce array,
Krishna imparts teachings, the cosmic play.
Dharma, duty, and paths to tread,
In Gita's verses, the soul is fed.

Amidst the warriors, with conch shells' sound,
Krishna unfolds truths, profound.
Duty without attachment, the essence clear,
In Krishna's words, there's naught to fear.

"Yoga of knowledge," the path of the sage,
Krishna guides Arjun on life's vast stage.
Detachment and devotion, a dual thread,
In Gita's verses, their essence spread.

The cosmic form revealed, a sight divine,
Krishna's glory, the eternal shrine.
From birth to death, the cycle turns,
In Krishna's wisdom, the seeker learns.

Through verses rhythmic, like a cosmic song,
Krishna and Arjun, their bond strong.
In the chariot of life, through joy and strife,
Gita's teachings, the elixir of life.

Duty fulfilled, with love's pure flame,
Krishna and Arjun, forever the same.
In the verses of Gita's sacred song,
A timeless wisdom, forever strong.

So, let the echoes of the Gita resound,
Krishna's teachings, forever profound.
In the battlefield of life, where challenges meet,
Bhagavad Gita, a guide, a retreat.

45. Krishna and Drona

On Kurukshetra's vast expanse, where warriors stood,
Krishna and Drona, in the battle's flood.
Dronacharya, a master of martial lore,
Krishna, the charioteer, their destinies swore.

In the art of war, Drona's skill profound,
A teacher, a guide, on battleground.
With bow in hand and an eagle eye,
Drona commands, the armies comply.

Yet, Krishna sees beyond the mortal veil,
In Drona's heart, where emotions sail.
A teacher torn by duty's might,
In Kurukshetra's field, the epic fight.

Duryodhana's ally, a martial sage,
Drona's loyalty on a fateful stage.
Krishna counsels, in wisdom's guise,
To tread the path where dharma lies.

In battles fierce, where arrows rain,
Drona's prowess, a relentless chain.
Krishna observes, the cosmic plan,
In the dance of war, where mortals stand.

Acharya Drona, with honor and pride,
Fights on Kaurava's side.
Krishna, the silent witness, knows,
The ebb and flow, where destiny flows.

As twilight casts its shadowy hue,
Drona's fate, a tale anew.
Krishna guides Arjun, a solemn call,
To end the charioteer's rise and fall.

In the cosmic play, where time unwinds,
Krishna and Drona, in destinies entwined.
A lesson profound in the battle's flow,
Where dharma and duty forever glow

46. Krishna and Ashwathama

On Kurukshetra's field, where destinies entwine,
A tale unfolds, of Krishna and Ashwathama's line.
A warrior fierce, with a darkened name,
Ashwathama, in the annals of war, his claim.

Krishna, the charioteer, with cosmic insight,
Witnesses the battles, in the day and night.
Ashwathama, a comet in the war's dark sky,
A force unleashed, with vengeance high.

In the battlefield's chaos, where warriors clash,
Ashwathama's prowess, like a thunderous flash.
Krishna observes, with a watchful eye,
In the cosmic drama, where destinies lie.

Drona's son, with a teacher's might,
Ashwathama's path, a shadowed light.
Krishna counsels Arjun, in the cosmic plan,
To face the challenges, as mortals can.

Yet, in the night's silence, a heinous act,
Ashwathama strikes, a dark impact.
Krishna witnesses, with a heavy heart,
The massacre, tearing the worlds apart.

In the aftermath, where sorrow prevails,
Ashwathama's deeds, the world bewails.
Krishna, the solace in the pain,
Guides Yudhishthir, in truth to regain.

The cosmic balance, in Krishna's hand,
Ashwathama's fate, a shifting sand.
In the epic's tapestry, where destinies weave,
A saga unfolds, in which both grieve.

So, in the verses of Kurukshetra's lore,
Krishna and Ashwathama, forevermore.
A lesson profound in the battle's flow,
Of choices made, in the ebb and glow.

47. Krishna and Shikhandi

In the pages of Mahabharata, a tale unfolds,
Of Krishna's wisdom and Shikhandi's courage, stories untold.

Shikhandi, born a princess, fate's intricate play,
A spirit unyielding, in a world astray.

Krishna, the charioteer, orchestrating fate's dance,
Navigating the cosmic script with a mystic glance.

On the battlefield of Kurukshetra, destiny entwined,
Shikhandi's presence, a turning of the cosmic mind.

With arrows and valor, the battle took its course,
Shikhandi, a force, driven by an inner force.

In the labyrinth of time, a warrior's soul reborn,
Championing truth, in the face of destiny's scorn.

Krishna, the divine strategist, a cosmic guide,
Whispering courage to Shikhandi at Kurukshetra's side.

As Arjuna's charioteer, Krishna's role defined,
Yet with Shikhandi's destiny, the cosmic script aligned.

Together they faced Bhishma, the grand patriarch,
A dance of fate, a symphony in the dark.

Shikhandi's arrows, a cascade of might,
Guided by Krishna, in the relentless fight.

In the echoes of war, a tale profound,
Krishna and Shikhandi, destiny unbound.

Their alliance, a testament to courage's call,
In the cosmic tapestry, they stand tall.

So, in the verses of time, let their saga be,
Of Krishna's guidance and Shikhandi's legacy.

48. Krishna and Sanjay

In the halls of Kurukshetra, where destinies unfold,
Sanjaya, the narrator, the epic story told.
A seer with vision, transcending the mundane,
In Krishna's presence, the cosmic terrain.

With a voice that echoed through the war's expanse,
Sanjaya's insight, a cosmic dance.
A witness to battles, where warriors strove,
In Krishna's guidance, the saga wove.

As Arjuna's charioteer, a sage so wise,
Sanjaya's words, a spiritual prize.
Through the Bhagavad Gita, his voice did soar,
In Krishna's teachings, a profound lore.

Krishna's discourse, a timeless guide,
In Sanjaya's words, truth did abide.
From the cosmic vision to life's profound quest,
Sanjaya's narrative, in Krishna's bequest.

In the midst of conflict, his vision clear,
Sanjaya narrated, without a fear.
Through the charioteer's eyes, he beheld,
Krishna's wisdom, a story unveiled.

The conch's mighty blow, the Panchajanya's sound,
Sanjaya's descriptions, in verses abound.
As Krishna guided, with words so divine,
Sanjaya's voice echoed through time.

The cosmic conversation, a philosophical sea,
Sanjaya's verses, like waves set free.
With Krishna's guidance, the warrior's plight,
In the Mahabharata's tapestry, a cosmic light.

Through the war's tumult, in Kurukshetra's breeze,
Sanjaya's words, a balm to appease.
A seer blessed, in Krishna's grace,
In every chapter, his words embrace.

So in the epic saga of Kurukshetra's fray,
Sanjaya's narrative, like a guiding ray.
In Krishna's presence, the timeless lore,
Sanjaya's voice, forevermore.

49. Krishna and Abhimanyu

In the sacred verses of Mahabharata's lore,
A chapter unfolds, of Krishna and Abhimanyu's core.

Krishna, the divine charioteer, wise and serene,
Guiding Arjuna through life's complex scene.

Abhimanyu, the valiant youth, with arrows bright,
Carrying the legacy, a radiant light.

In the panorama of Kurukshetra's vast array,
Krishna and Abhimanyu, their roles in the fray.

A bond beyond mentor, a cosmic connection,
Navigating destiny, in profound reflection.

The chakravyuha, a labyrinthine plight,
Abhimanyu's courage, a beacon in the night.

With inherited prowess and valor untold,
Into the circle of doom, the young warrior strolled.

Krishna's voice echoed, a celestial guide,
Navigating the maze where destinies hide.

In the midst of foes, a lone battle ensued,
Abhimanyu fought, his spirit imbued.

Yet, surrounded by adversaries in the fierce brawl,
A tragic end awaited, destiny's call.

Krishna, witnessing the youthful sacrifice,
Guided Arjuna through grief's cold ice.

In the echoes of Kurukshetra's war-torn land,
Krishna and Abhimanyu, a bond to withstand.

The chariot wheels turned, as time unwound,
A tale of valor, where destinies were bound.

In the annals of epic, their stories persist,
Krishna and Abhimanyu, in battles that exist.

50. Krishna and Dhritarashtra

In the corridors of Kurukshetra, where destiny's written,
Krishna and Dhritarashtra, their fates so smitten.

Dhritarashtra, the blind king, in his palace of gold,
Seeking power and control, a story of old.

Krishna, the divine charioteer, with a cosmic plan,
Guiding Arjuna through the chaos, a celestial span.

Dhritarashtra, in darkness, his vision obscured,
Yet within, a conflict, his conscience stirred.

Krishna, the harbinger of righteousness and truth,
Unfurling the dharma, with the grace of youth.

As the dice rolled in Hastinapura's grand hall,
Dhritarashtra's choices, like shadows, befall.

Krishna, the flute player, enchanting and wise,
Offering counsel, where destiny lies.

In the tapestry of Kurukshetra's vast plain,
Krishna and Dhritarashtra, their destinies in chain.

The blind king, torn by familial strife,
Krishna, the guide, offering a transformative life.

As war drums echoed and arrows took flight,
Dhritarashtra grappled with his inner plight.

Krishna, the charioteer, a beacon of light,
In the battlefield's chaos, where wrongs sought to smite.

Their paths intertwined in the cosmic embrace,
Krishna's wisdom, Dhritarashtra's internal space.

In the end, a kingdom lost, a dynasty's fall,
Yet lessons learned, as destiny's curtain did call.

So let the verses unfold their tale in rhyme,
Of Krishna and Dhritarashtra, in the sands of time.

51. Krishna and Gandhari

In the annals of Mahabharata, a saga unfolds,
Of Krishna's presence and Gandhari's story told.

Gandhari, a queen with a blindfolded sight,
Wrapped in darkness, yet radiating might.

Krishna, the divine charioteer of fate,
Navigating realms, where destinies conflate.

Gandhari's heart, a vessel of motherly love,
Yet destiny's design, like a storm above.

In Hastinapura's halls, where shadows loom,
Gandhari grapples with impending doom.

Krishna, the envoy of peace and cosmic balance,
Offers solace to Gandhari in her silent trance.

As Kauravas and Pandavas tread the path,
Krishna's guidance, a celestial aftermath.

Gandhari's eyes, veiled in eternal night,
Yet within, a maternal flame burning bright.

Krishna, the flutist, with melodies divine,
Whispers solace in Gandhari's troubled mind.

On Kurukshetra's plains, where destinies entwine,
Krishna and Gandhari, in the cosmic design.

Gandhari's sorrow, a river in silent flow,
Krishna, the consoler, with wisdom to bestow.

In the aftermath of war, where sorrow reigns,
Krishna and Gandhari, entwined in cosmic chains.

A tapestry woven with threads of fate,
Where Krishna's love and Gandhari's grief relate.

So let the verses sing of this cosmic rhyme,
Of Krishna and Gandhari, through the sands of time.

52. Krishna is Eternity

Beyond Dwarka's shores, where Krishna once reigned,
A cosmic chapter unfolded, destinies rearranged.

The city mourned, as tales of Krishna spread,
His earthly sojourn, a legacy widespread.

Yet in the hearts of devotees, Krishna lived on,
His teachings immortal, in the dawn and beyond.

As Dwarka wept, the waves whispered a tale,
Of a divine departure, where mortal senses fail.

The Gita's wisdom, a torch in the night,
Guiding seekers through life's cosmic flight.

In temples and hearts, Krishna's name resounds,
A celestial echo, where devotion abounds.

Radha, his consort, in love's eternal embrace,
Her devotion to Krishna, a celestial grace.

The flute, once played by Krishna's tender hand,
Echoed in the realms, where divine spirits stand.

The Yadavas, in sorrow, their heads hung low,
Yet Krishna's legacy continued to glow.

In Kurukshetra's echoes, in the hymns of the wise,
Krishna's essence endured, beyond earthly ties.

As time weaved its tapestry, Krishna's name,
A mantra of solace, in joy and in pain.

The tales of his leelas, in folklore they weave,
In the hearts of the faithful, where devotion grieves.

In the cosmic dance, where the eternal souls play,
Krishna's presence, a guiding light, beyond the fray.

So let the verses linger, in the realms unseen,
Of Krishna's legacy, in the cosmic sheen.

53. Krishna is Alive Forever

Upon Dwarka's shores, where waves gently kissed,
A chapter unfolded, by destiny's twist.

Krishna, Dwarkadhish, in divine splendor,
His time on Earth, now set to surrender.

The Yadavas, once united, now in discord,
A cosmic decree, by fate's swift sword.

As the Yadavas turned on each other in despair,
Krishna observed, his divine presence aware.

In the tumultuous sea, a hunter's stray dart,
A celestial arrow, piercing Krishna's heart.

The Lord of Dwarka, in a pose serene,
Ascended to heavens, no mortal scene.

The city wept, as tales of Krishna spread,
A divine departure, where tears were shed.

The flute now silent, the melodies hushed,
In Dwarka's twilight, in Krishna's legacy hushed.

Yet, beyond mortal coils, Krishna prevails,
In celestial realms, where eternity sails.

The Gita's wisdom, a guiding light,
In Krishna's absence, a celestial night.

His teachings linger, in the cosmic breeze,
A legacy enduring, as time appease.

In the tapestry of life, where stories unfold,
Krishna's departure, a tale foretold.

As the Yadavas grieved, and the world did sigh,
In the realm beyond, Krishna soared high.

So let the verses resonate, in sorrow's breath,
Of Krishna's transcendence, beyond life and death.

54. Krishna's Life After Mahabharat

Beyond the battlefield's dust, where echoes fade,
Krishna's journey transcends the war's cascade.

The war of righteousness, a tapestry woven,
Krishna, the charioteer, the saga is behoven.

In Dwarka's city, by the vast ocean's shore,
Krishna reigns, a divine presence evermore.

A flute in hand, the melodies resonate,
In the hearts of devotees, Krishna they contemplate.

As a king, Dwarkadhish, his rule so fair,
Guiding his kingdom with compassionate care.

Yet, destiny unfolds with an unpredictable thread,
The demise of Dwarka, where sorrows spread.

The Yadavas, once united, in discord divide,
Krishna watches, in wisdom, he confides.

Through the stormy seas and the tempest's wail,
Krishna's legacy, an immortal tale.

The sacred Gita, a scripture revered,
Guiding seekers, as wisdom is steered.

In his teachings, the essence of life,
Krishna's words, a balm in times of strife.

As the Yadavas witness a tragic fate,
Krishna's departure, a cosmic gate.

Amidst the banyan tree's sacred shade,
Krishna leaves, on a bed of flowers laid.

Ascending to the heavens, his divine abode,
Leaving behind tales, on the mortal road.

Yet in the hearts of devotees, Krishna remains,
His presence eternal, in celestial domains.

So let the verses echo, in time's embrace,
Of Krishna's legacy, transcending space.

55. Krishna and Hanuman

In the cosmic tapestry, where legends unfold,
Krishna and Hanuman, their stories told.
One, the Lord of Dwarka, divine and wise,
The other, a devotee with unwavering eyes.

In the sacred city of Dwarka's might,
Krishna reigns in celestial light.
Hanuman, with devotion profound,
In the heart's temple, his love is crowned.

Through Dwaraka's streets and Lanka's shore,
Krishna and Hanuman, a bond to explore.
In the Ramayana's pages, a tale so grand,
Hanuman serves, by Rama's command.

As Krishna's charioteer, in Kurukshetra's field,
Hanuman's presence, a blessing revealed.
Guiding Arjun with wisdom untold,
In the cosmic play, their destinies unfold.

In Rukmini's love and Radha's grace,
Krishna's heart, a sacred space.
Hanuman chants, in devotion's song,
In the divine chorus, where they both belong.

In the quest for Sita, and battles fought,
Hanuman and Krishna, in legends sought.
Through challenges faced and victories won,
Their stories echo, like the morning sun.

Hanuman leaps, with mountains in flight,
Krishna plays the flute, in the moonlit night.
A union of devotion, where hearts entwine,
In the cosmic dance, their spirits align.

So, in the verses of epics untold,
Krishna and Hanuman, their tales unfold.
In devotion's embrace and love's sweet song,
A bond eternal, forever strong.

56. Krishna's Wisdom: A Poetic Reflection

I am Krishna, the harbinger of light,
With wisdom that transcends the darkest night.
From the sacred lands of Mathura I hail,
Where love and knowledge forever prevail.

Within my being, the universe resides,
Echoing truths that the world often hides.
Through my flute's melody, hearts are stirred,
Awakening souls with each melodious word.

In the face of adversity, I stand tall,
Guiding humanity to rise above all.
With compassion as my guiding light,
I dispel ignorance, like the sun's might.

I am the whisper in the gentle breeze,
The solace amidst life's stormy seas.
Through devotion, I lead seekers astray,
Unveiling secrets in their spiritual way.

Embracing the dance of life's cosmic play,
I reveal the truth in my own unique way.
With each step, I ignite souls to ignite,
Shedding the veils of darkness, bringing forth light.

For those who seek, I am the eternal guide,
Nurturing hearts, illuminating the inside.

In each being, the divine spark I see,
Unveiling the truth of unity and harmony.

57. Krishna and Haridas Ji

In the sacred realms where devotion resides,
Haridas Ji, a soul whose love abides.
A saintly figure with a heart so pure,
In the cosmic dance, his soul did endure.

Haridas Thakur, a beacon of devotion,
A life immersed in divine emotion.
Born in a village, humble and small,
His love for God, the greatest call.

From an early age, his heart inclined,
To the holy names, his soul entwined.
Chanting and singing, in devotion's spree,
Haridas Ji, in love so free.

Rejected by society, for his lowly birth,
Haridas Ji found solace in God's worth.
In the secluded forest, his refuge he made,
In Krishna's love, his soul displayed.

The Maha Mantra, on his lips did flow,
A river of devotion, in its divine glow.
Harinam sankirtan, his sacred song,
In the heart of God, where he belonged.

Through the trials of life, Haridas stood,
His unwavering faith, like ancient wood.
Chanting the holy names, a timeless art,
In the rhythm of devotion, his beating heart.

Miracles unfolded in his sacred name,
Haridas Ji, a saint of divine fame.
With humility and love, his path was paved,
In the grace of God, his soul was saved.

From Jagannath Puri to the distant shore,
Haridas Ji's devotion, an endless lore.
A life dedicated to the holy sound,
In God's love, his essence found.

So in the realm of devotion's grace,
Haridas Ji, a saintly embrace.
Chanting the names, in devotion's sea,
His legacy echoes for eternity.

58. Krishna is Immortal

In the realm of tales, where legends unfurl,
A story of Krishna, a celestial pearl.
With his flute in hand, he danced and played,
A light-hearted melody his soul conveyed.

But fate took a twist, a somber turn,
As the prophecy whispered, causing hearts to yearn.
The end was nigh, destiny's decree,
A farewell to Krishna, a sight hard to see.

Yet in this sorrow, a light still shone,
For Krishna's death, not truly known.
A game they played, a divine disguise,
A chance for the Lord to mesmerize.

From the mortal realm, he seemed to depart,
But in truth, he resided deep in every heart.
His essence, eternal, forever alive,
Amidst the pain, a reason to revive.

His devotees, bewildered, shed their tears,
But Krishna's presence, still ever near.
With mischief in his eyes and laughter in his voice,
He reminded them to rejoice, to rejoice!

For death was just a charade, a cosmic jest,
A dance of illusion, a divine test.
Krishna's spirit, unbound and free,
A reminder to embrace life's jubilee.

So let us remember, in this light-hearted rhyme,
That death is but a moment, a fleeting chime.
For Krishna, the eternal, forever we adore,
His death a reminder, to live and love more.

59. Krishna and Kripalu Maharaj Ji

In the realms of devotion, where hearts align,
Kripalu Maharaj, a saintly design.
A beacon of love, in a world so vast,
In the cosmic dance, his soul did cast.

Born in Mangarh, a village serene,
Kripalu Maharaj, a saint unseen.
With a heart so pure, devotion's flame,
In God's love, his soul became.

Through the verses of bhajans sweet,
Kripalu Maharaj's devotion did greet.
A melodious hymn, in God's embrace,
His love echoed through time and space.

The wisdom profound in his teachings clear,
Kripalu Maharaj, a spiritual seer.
Through the path of devotion, his soul did tread,
In the footsteps of saints, where love is spread.

In Barsana's land, where Radha's name,
Kripalu Maharaj, his love did claim.
With Radha Krishna's eternal play,
In devotion's garden, he found his way.

Through the ashrams and the temple's gate,
Kripalu Maharaj, in love's estate.
With the grace of God, his teachings flowed,
In devotion's river, his soul rowed.

A message of love, compassion, and grace,
Kripalu Maharaj, in God's embrace.
Through selfless service and the joy of giving,
His love for God, forever living.

In the devotional songs and kirtans loud,
Kripalu Maharaj's love does crowd.
A saintly figure, in devotion's spree,
In the cosmic dance, eternally free.

So in the realms of love's grandeur,
Kripalu Maharaj, a saint so pure.
A soul immersed in devotion's lore,
In God's love, forevermore.

60. Krishna and Meera

In the realm of devotion, Meera shines bright,
A soul touched by love, a radiant light.
With devotion as her compass, she roams,
In search of the divine, she finds her home.
Her heart, a temple, where love resides,
In every breath, her devotion abides.
She sings with passion, her voice so clear,
Melodies of love that touch the ear.
Meera, a mystic, so full of grace,
Her love for Krishna, she can't erase.
Through trials and tribulations she'll go,
Her love for the divine, it continues to grow.
She dances with abandon, lost in ecstasy,
A soul entwined with the eternal, so free.
With every step, she transcends time,
In love's embrace, she finds the sublime.
Meera, an embodiment of devotion's fire,
Her love, a flame that will never tire.
She teaches us to surrender and let go,
To find liberation in love's eternal flow.
Oh Meera, your spirit inspires us all,
To answer love's divine call.
May we too find the path of devotion,
And experience love's true liberation.

61. Krishna and Radha Ramanji

In Vrindavan's sanctum, where devotion resides,
Radha Raman Ji, in love abides.
A deity divine, with enchanting charm,
In the heart of devotees, a sacred balm.

Adorned with peacock feathers, a celestial sight,
Radha Raman Ji, in eternal light.
With a flute in hand, and a gaze so sweet,
In the cosmic dance, his love does greet.

In the temple of Goswami Gopal Bhatt,
Radha Raman Ji, where hearts are caught.
A manifestation of Krishna's grace,
In devotion's sanctuary, a sacred space.

With eyes like lotus and a face so fair,
Radha Raman Ji, the soul's love affair.
In Radha's name, his essence weaves,
In the tapestry of love, where devotion cleaves.

Through the ages, his stories unfold,
Radha Raman Ji, a tale so bold.
Miracles whispered in devotion's ear,
In Vrindavan's aura, his presence clear.

With devotees singing in hymns of praise,
Radha Raman Ji, through devotion's maze.
In every bhajan and every prayer,
His divine presence, a love affair.

The sacred shila, where his form resides,
Radha Raman Ji, in love presides.
A symbol of love, in every hue,
In the cosmic dance, where love is true.

Through the fragrance of flowers and the temple's hymn,
Radha Raman Ji, in devotion's whim.
A deity adored, with love so rare,
In the heart of Vrindavan, he does declare.

So in the realms of devotion's spree,
Radha Raman Ji, eternally free.
A deity of love, in the cosmic lore,
In Vrindavan's heart, forevermore.

62. Krishna and Radha Vallabhacharya Ji

In the sacred haven where devotion blooms,
Radha Vallabhacharya, his love consumes.
A saintly figure, with a heart profound,
In the cosmic dance, his soul is found.

Born in Prayag, on the Ganga's shore,
Radha Vallabhacharya, his devotion bore.
In Vrindavan's embrace, his heart did soar,
A devotee of Radha, forevermore.

With verses sweet and hymns so pure,
Radha Vallabhacharya's love did endure.
In devotion's dance, his soul did play,
A devotee of Radha, in every way.

In the temple of Thakur Ji, he'd pray,
Radha Vallabhacharya, in devotion's sway.
Chanting the holy names, a sacred art,
In the rhythm of love, he found his part.

A lineage of devotion, in the Vallabh way,
Radha Vallabhacharya, a saint of the day.
Through philosophical teachings, profound and clear,
In Radha's love, his essence did appear.

With devotion's gaze and a heart so pure,
Radha Vallabhacharya, his love did assure.
In the sanctuary of Radha's grace,
His devotion found a sacred place.

Through the verses of poetry, his love did express,
Radha Vallabhacharya, in God's caress.
A devotee of Radha, in every breath,
In the cosmic dance, where devotion met.

So in the realms of devotion's spree,
Radha Vallabhacharya, eternally free.
A saintly soul in the cosmic lore,
In Radha's love, he found evermore.

63. Krishna and Narad Ji

In realms divine, where melodies play,
Narada, the celestial sage, finds his way.
Messenger of gods, with a veena in hand,
A cosmic minstrel, in every sacred land.

Born of mind-born creator's thought,
Narada's existence, divinely wrought.
A wandering sage, with no fixed abode,
In heavenly realms, his tales are stowed.

Veena's strings, tuned to cosmic hymns,
Resonate through worlds, where seraphim swim.
Messenger between realms, with wisdom adorned,
Narada, the troubadour, where secrets are scorned.

To Vaikuntha's gates, he often tread,
To Lord Vishnu, his devotion spread.
Chanting the names, a celestial choir,
Narada's devotion, a perpetual fire.

In tales of epics, his presence is traced,
In Mahabharata's weave, his wisdom graced.
From Brahma's boon to divine insight,
Narada's journey, an eternal flight.

A sage with humor, mischievous and wise,
Through cosmic tales, his essence lies.
Guiding kings and mendicants alike,
Narada's presence, a celestial hike.

Yet in his heart, a lesson profound,
Transcending time, his teachings resound.
In love for God, find eternal bliss,
Narada's message, a divine kiss.

Wandering through heavens and earthly climes,
Narada's presence, like poetic rhymes.
In the cosmic dance, a sage's part,
Narada, the eternal minstrel of the heart.

64. Krishna and Mahanbrata Brahmachari

In the realms of devotion, where saints reside,
Mahanbrata Brahmachari, with love as his guide.
A soul immersed in spiritual grace,
In the cosmic dance, his devotion does trace.

Born into the world with a celestial flame,
Mahanbrata Brahmachari, a saintly name.
A beacon of light, in devotion's hue,
In the sacred journey, his heart stayed true.

Through the path of Brahmacharya, so pure,
Mahanbrata's soul, in God's love did mature.
With celibacy as his sacred vow,
In devotion's garden, his spirit did plow.

In the footsteps of saints, his journey unfolds,
Mahanbrata Brahmachari, where love molds.
Through the verses of scriptures and hymns so sweet,
In the devotion's symphony, his soul did meet.

With every breath, a mantra divine,
Mahanbrata's devotion, like a sacred shrine.
In meditation's silence, his heart did soar,
In God's love, he found evermore.

Through the service to humanity's plight,
Mahanbrata Brahmachari, in love's light.
A selfless soul, with compassion so grand,
In devotion's embrace, his heart did stand.

In the temple of God, where silence sings,
Mahanbrata's devotion, like angelic wings.
A heart so pure, in meditation's trance,
In the cosmic dance, where spirits dance.

Through the trials of life and joyous days,
Mahanbrata Brahmachari, in devotion stays.
A soul entwined in love's embrace,
In the sacred journey, he finds his space.

So in the realms of devotion's grandeur,
Mahanbrata Brahmachari, a soul so pure.
A devotee whose heart aligns,
In God's love, eternally shines.

65. Krishna and Chaitanya Mahaprabhu

In ancient days of yore, in Bengal's sacred air,
A luminous soul emerged, divinely rare.
Chaitanya Mahaprabhu, a name that rings,
A saintly presence, from which devotion springs.

Born in Navadvipa, a town of grace,
In the year 1486, his divine embrace.
Nimai Pandit, his earthly name,
Yet destined for a celestial flame.

A scholar profound, with wisdom vast,
But within his heart, a yearning cast.
Seeking a truth, a higher plane,
He danced through life, transcending mundane.

In Gaya's sacred ground, a transformative trance,
A mystic encounter, a cosmic dance.
Lord Krishna's essence, a radiant glow,
In Chaitanya's heart, love began to flow.

The streets of Navadvipa echoed his call,
The holy names chanted, a spiritual thrall.
Kirtan's fervor, a joyous tide,
Devotees flocked, with hearts open wide.

Gauranga, they hailed, his divine form,
A golden avatar, through life's storm.
Sankirtan's waves, a melodic sea,
Chaitanya's presence, a sanctuary.

Through villages and towns, his message spread,
A path of love, where souls were led.
Bhakti's essence, pure and true,
Chaitanya's teachings, like morning dew.

With humility and love, he taught,
No barriers in devotion, all were sought.
Caste and creed, he cast aside,
In God's love, all could abide.

Through Jagannath Puri, he wandered on,
A pilgrimage of love, till life was gone.
Chaitanya Mahaprabhu, the soul's delight,
In every heart, a guiding light.

Five hundred years have passed, yet he remains,
In hearts of devotees, where love sustains.
Chaitanya's legacy, a spiritual stream,
A timeless tale, like a waking dream.

66. Krishna and Hridayan Ji

In the sanctuary of devotion, a heart beats strong,
Bhakti Hridayan, where love belongs.
A devotee whose heart is a shrine,
In the cosmic dance, his love does shine.

With every breath, a mantra sweet,
Bhakti Hridayan's devotion, a sacred beat.
In the temple of love, where emotions play,
His heart aligns, in devotion's sway.

Through the verses of bhajans and hymns,
Bhakti Hridayan's love begins.
A melody of devotion, pure and bright,
In the realm of God's love, his soul takes flight.

With each prayer and every vow,
Bhakti Hridayan, in devotion bow.
In the cosmic tapestry, where love is spun,
His heart's devotion, forever run.

Through the trials of life and joyous days,
Bhakti Hridayan, in devotion stays.
A soul entwined in love's embrace,
In the sacred journey, he finds his space.

In the echoes of kirtans and the temple's bell,
Bhakti Hridayan's devotion does swell.
A river of love, in God's domain,
In the cosmic dance, where emotions reign.

Through the verses of scriptures and holy text,
Bhakti Hridayan's devotion is complex.
A tapestry of faith and love so bright,
In the heart of devotion, his spirit takes flight.

So in the realms of love's grandeur,
Bhakti Hridayan, a soul so pure.
A devotee whose heart aligns,
In God's love, eternally shines.

67. Krishna and Surdas Ji

In the realms of devotion, a poet emerged,
Surdas ji, with verses where Krishna's love surged.

Blind in the mortal gaze, yet sight profound,
His heart, a temple, where devotion is crowned.

Krishna, the divine, the flutist so sweet,
In Surdas ji's verses, their spirits would meet.

In the bylanes of Braj, where stories unfurl,
Surdas ji sang, his heart a lyrical swirl.

Krishna's tales, a symphony in Surdas ji's song,
In the cosmic dance, where they both belong.

With a soulful gaze, beyond earthly sight,
Surdas ji envisioned Krishna's celestial light.

In the embrace of Vrindavan's sacred ground,
Krishna and Surdas ji, a communion profound.

The blind poet's verses, a river divine,
Flowing with love for the Lord of time.

Krishna, the muse, in Surdas ji's song,
Their connection eternal, in verses strong.

Through melodies sweet, and devotion deep,
Surdas ji's hymns, like whispers in sleep.

In Krishna's presence, Surdas ji found,
A love unbound, a celestial surround.

The heart's yearning, in each rhythmic line,
A poetic journey, where divinity intertwine.

So let the verses echo through time's expanse,
Of Surdas ji's devotion, in Krishna's dance.

68. Krishna and Rasdas Ji

In the heart of Braj, where devotion flows,
Rasdas Ji, a saintly spirit chose.
A devotee whose love knew no bounds,
In the cosmic dance, his soul resounds.

Born in the village of Pichhor,
Rasdas Ji's devotion began to soar.
A life dedicated to Krishna's grace,
In the realms of love, he found his place.

In the village's fields and rustic air,
Rasdas Ji's devotion laid bare.
Through every challenge and life's quest,
His love for Krishna, a sacred zest.

With verses composed in the praise of God,
In Rasdas Ji's words, devotion awed.
Bhajans and hymns, his soul did sing,
In Krishna's love, eternal spring.

Through the forests of Braj, where peacocks dance,
Rasdas Ji's devotion, a divine trance.
In the echo of his lyrical song,
A devotee's journey, so strong.

His poetry spoke of love's sweet fire,
In Krishna's love, his heart did aspire.
Through Radha's eyes, the divine gaze,
Rasdas Ji's verses, a celestial phase.

In the temple of Govind Dev Ji,
Rasdas Ji's devotion flowed free.
Through the beats of the mridanga's drum,
In the cosmic dance, his soul did hum.

With every breath and every beat,
Rasdas Ji's devotion, a melody sweet.
In the company of saints, his heart aligned,
In Krishna's love, his spirit shined.

So in the realm of devotion's spree,
Rasdas Ji, a devotee so free.
Through verses and hymns, his love did soar,
A soul entwined in Krishna's lore.

69. Ode to Krishna Devotees

In the realm where devotion blooms,
Where the heart's purest essence resumes,
There walk the souls, steadfast and true,
Who seek the path of moksha through.

With eyes fixed on the eternal light,
They tread the path, both day and night,
Sacrificing all worldly ties,
For the divine that never dies.

In Krishna's name, they find their song,
A melody that's deep and strong,
Each step they take, a humble prayer,
For grace and love beyond compare.

Their lives, a testament of faith,
Unwavering in joy or wraith,
In every breath, in every sigh,
They whisper, "Krishna," reaching high.

Through trials fierce and nights so long,
They hold to Him, their spirit's song,
For bhakti's path is theirs to tread,
With Krishna's love, they're gently led.

To you, O devotees so pure,
Whose hearts in Krishna's love endure,
May your journey bring you peace,
And in His light, may you release.

For in your sacrifice, we see,
A boundless love, eternally,
In Krishna's arms, you'll find your rest,
Forever blessed, forever blessed.

70. Gopal, Our Hearts Delight

In temples grand, where candles gleam,
Devotees gather, hearts agleam,
With tear-streaked faces, they implore,
For Krishna's love, they yearn for more.

In fervent prayers, their voices rise,
Echoing through the starlit skies,
"Bring us Gopal," their hearts do plea,
"A child divine, our joy to see."

With tiny steps and playful grace,
They see him in each sacred space,
In murtis crafted with devotion pure,
They feel his presence, love secure.

Like parents dear, their arms extend,
To cradle Krishna, hearts to mend,
In every smile, in every tear,
They find their Gopal, ever near.

O Krishna, come, their souls beseech,
With every breath, your name they reach,
In temples grand and homes so small,
Your love, their life, their one and all.

For in your childlike, divine embrace,
They find their solace, joy, and grace,
O Gopal dear, their hearts' delight,
You are their morning, noon, and night.

The Last Note

As you turn the final page of "The Divine Circle: A Poetic Journey of Krishna and His Companions," I hope you have felt the same sense of wonder, devotion, and love that inspired these poems. The timeless stories of Krishna and his beloved companions have a unique ability to touch our hearts and souls, transcending the boundaries of time and space.

Through their eyes and words, we gain insights into the profound teachings and miracles of Krishna, and we are reminded of the boundless love and devotion that defined their lives. It is my sincere hope that this collection has brought you closer to the divine essence of Krishna and has enriched your understanding of his timeless wisdom.

Thank you for embarking on this poetic journey with me. May the stories and emotions captured in these poems continue to inspire and guide you on your own path.

With heartfelt gratitude,
Ravindra Singh Thakur

About the Author

Ravindra Singh Thakur is a joyful and passionate individual born in Sehore and currently residing in Dewas. He completed his Electrical Engineering degree from Oriental University in Indore, Madhya Pradesh, and is employed in India's leading Edtech industry. Ravindra's love for writing sparked at a young age, especially when he delved into the stories of Bhagat Singh and Veer Savarkar. Inspired by these tales, he felt compelled to express himself through writing and penned his first poem with the guidance of his teachers after completing class 12.

For Ravindra, every person, whether alive or deceased, serves as a wellspring of inspiration that propels him forward in his literary pursuits. His ultimate goal has always been to be a good person and utilize his writings in various forms to spread literature. Ravindra's writing journey has been eventful, with his participation in 30+ anthologies. Additionally, he holds the esteemed position of editor for the Hindi anthology "कुछ अनकहे से अल्फ़ाज़" and has authored three eBooks: "वो सात दिन," "World of Women and Contemporary Stories," and "स्वयंसेवक एक देशभक्त."

Ravindra's literary accomplishments extend beyond anthologies and eBooks. He has penned the novel "Twirls and Twists: Friendship VS Love" and curated a collection of six stories titled "Benevolent Analects." Currently, he is engrossed in writing other novels based on captivating retro stories, set to be published in both Hindi and eBook formats. Moreover, Ravindra has authored a pocket book called "A Stranger Story" and actively contributes as an audiobook writer on KukuFM.

Acknowledging his talent and dedication, Ravindra has garnered three awards for his debut novel. He received recognition as one of India's top 100 best inspirational authors by The Indian Awaz, secured a spot among the top 100 debut authors in India as honored by Literature's Light, and was celebrated as one of the top 50 influential authors in the country by The Spirit Mania. Furthermore, he has been nominated for various upcoming awards in 2020, adding to his growing list of accolades.

Ravindra Singh Thakur's passion, unwavering dedication, and remarkable talent make him an exceptional writer and an inspiration to others. His contributions to the literary world have earned him well-deserved recognition, solidifying his status as a prominent figure in the writing community.

Connect with Ravindra Singh Thakur:
- Instagram: [@authorravin](https://instagram.com/authorravin)
- Facebook: [@authorravin](https://www.facebook.com/authorravin)
- Website: www.ravindrasinghthakur.com
- Twitter: [@authorravin](https://twitter.com/authorravin)

www.ingramcontent.com/pod-product-compliance
Lightning Source LLC
LaVergne TN
LVHW010108170826
845678LV00012B/2300
* 9 7 8 8 1 9 6 7 1 2 4 9 5 *